C000059331

CLONING

AND

STEM CELL RESEARCH

by
Anthony McCarthy

*All booklets are published thanks to the
generous support of the members of the
Catholic Truth Society*

CATHOLIC TRUTH SOCIETY
PUBLISHERS TO THE HOLY SEE

CONTENTS

Introduction 4

Scientific Background 6

Church Teaching 22

Examining the Arguments 35
    Cloning for birth 35
    Cloning for research/transplantation 58

Glossary 72

Further Reading 80

The Author

Anthony McCarthy is Research Fellow at the Linacre Centre and holds an M.A. in Philosophy from King's College London. He is currently engaged in doctoral studies at St Mary's College, University of Surrey.

Acknowledgements

I wish to thank Peter Garrett of LIFE for allowing me to make use of his research material and Dr Helen Watt and Professor David Prentice for their comments on the text.

THE LINACRE CENTRE

The Linacre Centre is the only Catholic institution of its kind specialising in the field of healthcare ethics in Great Britain and Ireland. As such it provides a unique service to the Catholic community in these islands and more particularly to Catholics working in the field of healthcare. The Centre also exists to assist the teaching authorities within the Church in addressing bioethical issues, and to communicate and defend the Church's moral teaching in debates over public policy and legislation in the United Kingdom.

The Centre has built up a large bioethics library at the Hospital of St John and St Elizabeth in London. It has three fulltime research fellows who are able to give time and thought to new and difficult issues in bioethics and it is also able to call upon the help of a range of experts in medicine, law, philosophy, theology and history. The Centre is affiliated to Ave Maria School of Law, Ann Arbor, Michigan. It publishes reports, organises conferences and lectures, and does consultancy work for individuals and for other organisations. The co-operation of the Linacre Centre in publishing the *CTS Explanations* series of booklets is intended to advance this work of providing clear Catholic teaching on bioethical issues.

INTRODUCTION

Modern medicine and medical research have ever increasing power to benefit the human race. But medicine and science can be carried out in ways not beneficial to humanity. They can be used to treat disease, but they can equally be used to benefit the few at the cost of the many, or the powerful at the expense of the weak.

The way in which medical knowledge/technology should be used is an ethical rather than a technical question. Ethical questions are questions about how we, as human persons, should mould our behaviour in order to achieve what is truly good for us and avoid what is bad. Medical and scientific knowledge cannot provide answers to these questions. Only by paying attention to what we as human beings *are*; what our needs are; what is fulfilling of our nature; can we hope to come to an understanding of the principles that should guide technology and medicine.

Human cloning is frequently presented as an impending scientific achievement, with potential medical applications. The aim of this booklet is to describe what human cloning is, examine its ethical status, and analyse what it will mean for us. The booklet is divided into a largely factual chapter describing the science of cloning and stem cell research, a chapter on the Church's teaching with regard to human cloning and procreation, and a chapter examining philosophical arguments both for and against human cloning.

SCIENTIFIC BACKGROUND

Cloning

Cloning means the production of a living being that is genetically identical to the one from which it originated. Specifically, human cloning is the artificial production of a **genetic replica**[1] of another human being. This is achieved without the contribution of two **gametes** (sperm and ovum), and is therefore a form of **asexual reproduction**. Whereas **IVF** is a form of reproduction achieved by fertilisation of an ovum (egg) by a sperm outside the body, sperm is not used in cloning.

In normal human fertilisation, the fusion between sperm and ovum produces a **zygote** (embryo at the one-cell stage), with a complement of 46 **chromosomes**, 23 from each parent. This is how each of us started life. The zygote is **diploid** genetically (has a full set of 46 chromosomes), having received a **haploid** set of 23 chromosomes from the mother and father.

Cloning attempts, one way or another, to bypass fertilisation by using a full diploid set of genes to program development. Described below are two procedures which could be used for attempting human cloning.

[1] The first time a technical term is used it will appear in bold. The glossary at the back of the booklet gives definitions of these terms.

Cloning by embryo splitting[2]

The cells of an embryo in its earliest stages of development are **totipotent**. This means that they are capable of producing any human tissue or organ, or even a separate human being if the cells are isolated from the original embryo. By subdividing (splitting) an embryo at this stage, a clone or clones of the embryo can be produced. It would appear that the original embryo is destroyed in this process. Human **embryo splitting** has thus far resulted in a very high mortality rate among the embryos produced and this method of cloning looks as though it has little future. This procedure of artificially induced twinning could not produce a clone of an adult human being. Given the above, all future references to cloning, unless otherwise specified, will refer to the second method known as **somatic cell nuclear transfer**.

Cloning by somatic cell nuclear transfer

In order for cloning to take place, the nucleus of an unfertilised ovum is removed and replaced with the nucleus of a **somatic cell**, or whole diploid body cell, from a developed embryo, foetus or adult individual. The ovum is then stimulated either chemically or by an electrical pulse to create a human embryo. Given that the nucleus contains almost all of a cell's genetic material,

---

[2] Sometimes known as 'twin fission'.

the new embryo will be a delayed genetic twin/clone of the human individual from whom the cell was taken. In this whole process male sexuality plays no direct role.

The clone will not be an exact genetic copy of the individual cloned, because there are some genes (about 0.05% of the human **genome**), located in the ovum but outside the nucleus. These are called **mitochondrial** genes and their existence ensures a slight genetic difference between the clone individual and the cell donor (unless the cell donor and ovum donor are one and the same individual). The very procedure of cloning may also cause genetic changes other than those that occur naturally in a growing embryo.

In 1996/7 a team of scientists from the Roslin Institute in Scotland succeeded in cloning a sheep, implanting the clone embryo into another sheep's uterus, and bringing the clone to birth. The clone was named Dolly. Before their attempt to clone an adult ewe using one of her body cells, the same Institute had found a way of cloning developed sheep embryos by using their quiescent embryonic cells. This method was then applied using quiescent adult cells. Adult cell nuclei (e.g. skin cell nuclei) become **specialised** by selectively switching off the genes they contain which are not relevant to their particular function. The Roslin scientists took adult cells from an sheep's udder, and were able to make the nuclei of mature specialised cells **unspecialised**, thereby restoring the instructive potential of the full complement of genes in the nucleus, or 'switching-on' the majority of previously 'switched-off' genes.

The success rates of the technique in Dolly's case were very low. From the fusion of 277 **enucleated** ova (ova which had had their nuclei removed) with somatic cell nuclei, only 29 embryos were created and transferred to sheep. Of these, only one made it to birth. Thus far, there has been little improvement on these results for clone animals. It has become clear that the setting back to zero of a cell's specialisation process has not been fully achieved, and that the DNA in the cell from which Dolly was formed continued to age. Dolly has since been put down after a veterinary examination revealed that she had a progressive lung disease found primarily in aged sheep. The overwhelming majority of clones or attempted clones created by somatic cell nuclear transfer have either been entities with no developmental potential, or embryos with severe genetic abnormalities which can miscarry at any stage of pregnancy. Many of those born have suffered disabilities or become oversized, a condition known as **large offspring syndrome** (LOS). Whether human clones would be likely to suffer from LOS is much disputed.

It should also be noted that there have been attempts to transfer human cell nuclei into enucleated animal ova. In one experiment a human cell nucleus was fused with an enucleated pig ovum, resulting in an entity which developed in a similar fashion to a human embryo up to about 32 cells, after which it was discarded.

Parthenogenesis

Parthenogenesis has been called a form of cloning but is in fact something different. The term refers to the production of an embryo from an unfertilised ovum without the injection of a donor cell or nucleus. This occurs naturally in some non-mammal species. Nothing is cloned here, for no body cell is used as a template for replication. Some scientists have proposed radically changing the makeup of an ovum so that embryonic development could take place using only the genetic material from the ovum itself. This would be done by chemically treating an ovum to induce it to keep its entire set of chromosomes and to develop as an embryo. The genetic makeup of an ovum, as it matures, is **randomised**, so any individual formed through parthenogenesis would be genetically different from its mother. The new individual would be far more genetically distinct from the mother than a clone would be from its adult cell donor.

Possible reasons for abnormalities in clones

In human sexual reproduction the chromosomal DNA of sperm and egg cells are specialised during their maturation so that at fertilisation both sets of DNA are ready for the specific pattern of gene expression required for normal embryo development. This process is called **reprogramming**, and is thought to occur via **genetic imprinting**. Most of the thousands of genes a person inherits come in two copies, one from each parent. When an embryo is conceived in the usual way, the father's and mother's genes are chemically 'imprinted', so that only one will be active. Imprinting is a process in which one of the two copies of a gene is switched off.

When an embryo is created by cloning, it is not clear how this imprinting and reprogramming process works, since DNA from only one individual is present. Somatic cells have a very different internal structure to sperm, and it is necessary for all reprogramming of the transferred nucleus to occur within hours or even minutes of activation of the restructured ovum. Incomplete reprogramming will lead to abnormalities in overall gene expression, and the failure of the embryo or foetus to develop, or to developmental abnormalities in those that survive. Although there is still much uncertainty in this area, it is thought that cloning usually fails in animals because there is not enough time for full reprogramming to occur.

Purposes of cloning

Outlined above are descriptions of two technical procedures used to carry out cloning. Both techniques, if successfully applied to human individuals, will produce

a new human being at its embryonic stage of
development. This makes it clear that *all* human cloning
is, in fact, reproductive. The term 'reproductive cloning'
is therefore a tautology.

Aside from the definition of cloning as a technical
procedure, it has become commonplace to define cloning
in terms of the purposes for which it is done. These
'definitions by aim', need to be carefully analysed.
Nowadays there is much talk of "reproductive cloning"
and "therapeutic cloning", as though they were different
types of cloning. They are not. "Therapeutic cloning"
refers to the production by cloning of a human embryo
for the purpose of using that individual as a source of
cells or for experimentation that may offer therapeutic
benefits to other human beings. The term is manipulative
because it obscures the fact that such interventions
carried out on the early clone human embryo are never
therapeutic for that individual, who, as a result of having
cells extracted from it at an early stage, will die.

For the sake of clarity, and given the fact that all
cloning is reproductive in itself, this booklet will refer
to **cloning for research/transplantation** (or
experimental cloning), and **cloning for birth** (or **live-
birth cloning**). In the term 'cloning for birth' is
included both cloning done with the intention to implant
and bring to birth, and also any implantation of a clone
embryo for this purpose.

Cloning for birth

An example of cloning for birth has been given with the case of Dolly the sheep. In a human case it would mean implanting a clone embryo in the uterus of a woman whose ovum had been used for cloning, or in the uterus of a **surrogate mother**, with the intention that the clone child be carried to term. This new individual human being, barring genetic mutation, should produce a body structure similar to that of its adult cell donor. Cloning for birth has, among other things, been proposed as a way for women suffering from infertility to obtain clone children. These children, commissioned by and cloned from the infertile woman, would be produced using another woman's ovum, then implanted, gestated and born through either the **commissioning mother** or a surrogate.

Given what we presently know from animal cloning, it is clear that this procedure would cause physical harm to human clones. Indeed, recent research on rhesus monkeys suggests that human cloning may not be able to produce viable human offspring. If offspring were to be created many would have severe genetic or other disabilities, which might only become apparent at late stages of pregnancy. Many babies would miscarry and those making it to birth would be likely to suffer premature death or major health problems caused by the means used to produce them. Nearly all scientists working in the field would accept this. On top of these problems, clone human beings who were discovered in the womb to be disabled would be at a much higher risk of being destroyed through deliberate abortion.

Women choosing to gestate clone children would be exposed to grave physical and psychological harm. The high rate of miscarriage would carry health risks for the mother, aside from the trauma that would result from either miscarriage or neonatal death. Observation of animal clones has shown that malformed or oversized foetuses could constitute a direct physical threat to the **gestational mother**. In such cases as these, as well as in cases of genetic disability, mothers would be under pressure to abort the child they were carrying. Abortion, in addition to taking the life of the child, would carry health risks for the mother, both physical and psychological. It has also been pointed out that mothers of clones could be at risk from **choriocarcinoma**, a form of cancer unique to humans, which develops from the **trophoblast** (the part of the embryo that attaches to the womb wall and develops into the **placenta**). It seems that genes linked to the development of the placenta remain 'switched-on' after reprogramming in clones, and any acceleration in the growth of the placenta could pose high risks for the mother.

Cloning for research/transplantation

Successful human cloning always results in the production of a new human individual, with a pre-set genetic patrimony. In cloning for research/transplantation this human individual is created as a means to a medical or scientific end. The aim may be to obtain organs, tissue or cells of a required genetic quality. Although the common proposals of research scientists in this area concern pre-implantation embryos, some propose that the human clone should, for these same purposes, be implanted and grown in a womb, then aborted. This proposal still comes under the category of cloning for research/transplantation. The aim in some cases may also be to observe embryonic development in order to understand the genetic mechanisms of cell growth, differentiation etc.

In the cases commonly proposed, further development of the human embryo would be halted before implantation, when the embryo is 5-7 days old (sometimes called the **blastocyst** stage). At this stage, the human embryo's cells, because unspecialised, have the capacity to produce many different types of cell. Such cells are **embryonic stem cells** and are **pluripotent**. This distinguishes them from earlier totipotent cells, which are capable of forming any other type of cell, or of producing a separate organism. In order to isolate the pluripotent cells from an embryo's inner cell mass the embryo is destroyed.

Stem cells

Each new embryo has to generate all of the cells of the adult it could become, and those cells must be organised into a functionally integrated whole. **Stem cells** play a central role in this process. The term 'stem cell' is used to refer to *any* cell that is able to reproduce itself and to produce specialised cells for various tissues in the body. There are many of these versatile stem cells in the body at various stages of development. It is therefore important to note that as well as embryonic stem cells, there are stem cells, known as **adult stem cells**, that arise later in development and can be found in specific tissue. The term embryonic stem cell is often used to include cells from very late embryos and foetuses, as well as early embryos. The term adult stem cell is used to refer to stem cells found in specific tissue that arise at later stages such as in a newborn baby.

Certain medical conditions such as **Alzheimer's**, **Parkinson's**, **Motor Neurone disease**, diabetes, spinal cord injury and diseases of the heart are said to be either currently or potentially treatable with the use of stem cells.

Embryonic stem cells

Embryonic stem cells can be obtained from an embryo or foetus after miscarriage, early abortion, or from embryos created through IVF. They may also be obtained from embryos created specifically for experimental use, either through IVF or cloning.

Scientists discovered some time ago that by isolating individual embryonic stem cells and maintaining them in **culture** they would continue to divide indefinitely. Such isolated cells are known as **embryonic stem cell lines**.

While these cells divide, they do not do so in the co-ordinated way that defines embryonic development. They may even in certain conditions form malignant tumours (known as **teratomas**). However, provided with appropriate **molecular signals**, these cells can be coaxed to generate a huge number of mature cell types. It is an unresolved question whether these mature cell types in culture (e.g. a brain cell) are capable of assimilating into the structure of a developed organ (e.g. a brain), without bringing with them the risk of malignant tumours. Tumours can occur because the mature cells, once transplanted, have a tendency to revert back to their embryonic state and grow in a completely uncontrolled fashion. Similar problems also seem to apply to early **foetal cells**. A case has been recorded of a man with Parkinson's disease dying after receiving a transplant of foetal cells. It was found that these cells had given rise to bone, skin and hair in the patient's brain.

In this context it is worth noting that the only positive results recorded from the use of embryonic stem cells thus far are those involving foetal cells. It is questionable whether these cells should even be referred to as embryonic.

Human embryonic stem cell lines in existence at present are either not growing well or are difficult to control, and there is fear that their properties will degrade with time. A further problem with the use of embryonic stem cells lies in

the fact that any **immune system** will eventually try and
destroy transplanted cells. As with organ transplantation,
the speed of this destruction will be dependent on the
closeness of the match between donor and recipient. The
use of clones has been proposed as a way round this
problem. However, there are a number of difficulties with
this. Firstly, even early embryonic cells (whether from
clones or not) have surface molecules capable of causing an
immune response. Secondly, as animal cloning
experiments have demonstrated, the vast majority of these
clones are likely to have cells which are genetically
abnormal. Thus far, animal experiments have provided little
evidence that cells generated from embryonic stem cells can
be safely transplanted back into adult animals for restorative
purposes. On a practical level, the lack of availability of
women's eggs, combined with the low efficiency of the
cloning process, makes it difficult to see how cloning for
embryonic stem cells could become a standard procedure.

It remains to be seen what potential therapeutic
benefits might be derived from the use of embryonic stem
cells. All we can say for certain is that at present there are
serious limitations to their potential usefulness.

Adult stem cells

While it has been known for many years that there are stem
cells present in adult tissue, until recently it was assumed
that they could only form cells of a particular type of

tissue. However, transplantation experiments on animals have shown that stem cells derived from a particular tissue can develop into cells of a completely different type. In recent years versatile stem cells have been discovered in a variety of human tissue, including bone marrow, spinal cord, brain, connective tissue of various organs, and in the blood of the umbilical cord. These adult stem cells can go on to form a number of cell types, including blood, muscle and nerve cells. The cells can be extracted by **tissue biopsy** on patients, and then grown in culture. From here they can be induced to differentiate into a wide range of mature cell types. Recent research has shown that adult stem cells isolated from the marrow of mice, rats and people can be transformed into cells of blood, gut, liver, lung, brain, and other parts of the body. Included in this research is evidence that adult stem cells from bone marrow have a unique **immunity tolerance**.

Prior to these recent discoveries, adult stem cells from bone marrow and umbilical cord had been used in transplants for years. The use of versatile adult stem cells has already produced positive results in humans. In 2001 a cardiac infarct patient was treated with stem cells from his own body. Stem cells from the patient's own bone marrow, after injection into the patient, are thought to have autonomously converted into heart muscle, leading to improvements in the severely damaged heart. Successful treatments of blood diseases, **Crohn's**

disease and some rare skin diseases have also been recorded. In these treatments, a direct infusion from the patient or a donor is used, and no modification is made to turn stem cells into particular tissue. Many forms of leukemia, as well as other diseases, have been successfully treated in this way. Scientists are agreed that the ideal cells for transplant are those deriving from the patient. This is because when the cells are from the same body, there is no risk of rejection. Such cells are also incapable of forming the kind of tumours that embryonic stem cells may form.

Some argue that adult stem cells are more specialised than embryonic stem cells, and therefore less capable of generating a full range of mature tissue. However, this remains unclear, and research coming from the University of Minnesota has suggested that at least some adult stem cells are pluripotent. Moreover, even if adult stem cells are more specialised than their embryonic counterparts, this very specialisation could be advantageous. As neurobiologist Maureen Condic has pointed out, a completely unspecialised stem cell requires many steps in order to become specialised, and each step has to be a correct one if the cell is to become the type intended. A partly specialised cell has fewer steps to go in order to become the type desired. While this might mean that a particular adult stem cell has fewer applications than an embryonic counterpart, a set of adult stem cells from different stem cell populations could well be capable of forming any other type of cell, and in a way guaranteed to be more successful.

Nobody knows how successful adult stem cells will ultimately prove to be, but we can be confident that they will be useful, because they have already yielded positive results when used in treatments for human patients.

CHURCH TEACHING

What does the Catholic Church teach with regard to human cloning? A number of statements have been made by popes and by the Congregation for the Doctrine of the Faith (CDF) with regard to reproductive technology and cloning. These statements must be seen in the light of the Church's teaching with regard to the sanctity of life, the status of the embryo, and the meaning of sex and marriage.

Status of the embryo

The Church's *Instruction on Respect for Human Life in its Origin and on the Dignity of Procreation [Donum Vitae]* (1987), The *Catechism of the Catholic Church* (1994), and the papal encyclical *The Gospel of Life [Evangelium Vitae]* (1995) teach unmistakably that the moment a zygote is formed it is owed the unconditional respect morally due to a human person. In 1987 the CDF, with Pope John Paul II's approval, declared: "From the time that the ovum is fertilised, a new life is begun which is neither that of the father nor of the mother; it is rather the life of a new human being with his own growth. It would never be made human if it were not human already." The Congregation further states: "...the fruit of human generation from the first moment of its existence, that is to say, from the moment the zygote has formed, demands the unconditional respect that is morally due to the human being in his bodily and spiritual totality. Since the embryo must be treated as a person, it must also be defended in its integrity. [I.1]"

Quoting from *Donum Vitae*, Pope John Paul II repeats in *Evangelium Vitae* that "the human embryo is to be respected and treated as a person from the moment of conception." In *Evangelium Vitae*, the Pope clarifies that the Church has taught infallibly that abortion is seriously wrong, and solemnly declares that: "direct abortion, that is abortion willed as an end or as a means, always constitutes a grave moral disorder, since it is the deliberate killing of an innocent human being. [62]"

The historical record shows that the Church's teaching that abortion is a grave moral evil has been, in the words of one scholar, 'clear, emphatic and unwavering'[3]. The *Didache* (c.80), the oldest known source of ecclesiastical law, enjoins that: "You shall not slay the child by abortion." Two early Church councils - of Elvira in Granada, Spain (c.305) and of Ancyra in Galatia, Asia Minor (314) further condemned abortion, setting a precedent which later councils ratified and strengthened. The attitude of the Church to the unborn contrasted strongly with the prevalent pagan attitude, which both permitted and encouraged abortion and infanticide.

---

[3] The Roman Catholic Church and Abortion: An Historical Perspective, Professor D. DeMarco, Homiletic and Pastoral Review July 1994.

The Old and New Testaments continuously affirm the goodness and value of life. We are urged to: "...choose life, that you and your descendants may live, loving the Lord your God, obeying his voice and cleaving to Him; for that means life to you and length of days, that you may dwell in the land which the Lord swore to your fathers, to Abraham, to Isaac and to Jacob, to give them." (*Deuteronomy* 30:19-20). The great value attaching to every single human being is emphasised again and again in the Bible. Psalm 8 states: "what is man that thou art mindful of him and the son of man that thou dost care for him? Yet thou hast made him little less than God, and dost crown him with glory and honour." In the New Testament, the Annunciation of Christ's conception in the Virgin Mary's womb; the subsequent rejoicing of the unborn John the Baptist a week or two after at the Visitation and Elizabeth's greeting of Mary as "the mother of my Lord", give compelling witness to the sanctity of life from the moment of conception.

The sanctity of human life and the nature of the person are reaffirmed in the *Catechism of the Catholic Church*, which states that: "The human *body* shares in the dignity of the image of God: it is a human body precisely because it is animated by a spiritual soul, and it is the whole human person that is intended to become, in the body of Christ, a temple of the Spirit (364)". The Church here makes clear that the human being is not, as some have held, two distinct realities: a person (soul) and a sub-personal body. Rather, a human being is a dynamic unity of body, mind and spirit. The Church has traditionally understood the human soul as the unifying form of the human organism. The human body, far from being mere matter, is irreducibly part of the personal reality of the human being. The value and dignity of the human body are therefore inherent to it.

With the Incarnation, God Himself, in the Second Person of the Trinity, became a human being of flesh and blood (*John* 1:14), suffered bodily and rose from the dead bodily. Christ's life, death and resurrection, in fully revealing man to himself, underlines the dignity of human bodily life in all its forms.

The *Catechism of the Catholic Church* states: "The Church teaches that every spiritual soul is created immediately by God - it is not "produced" by the parents - and also that it is immortal: it does not perish when it separates from the body at death, and it will be reunited with the body at the final Resurrection (366)". Thus human beings are not only works of nature, but also unique creations of God *ex nihilo*, in which God is involved from the very beginning. Each of us is created in His very image (*Genesis* 1:26-27). This is true of all human beings, whether they come to be by means of the marital act or via cloning, IVF, fornication, adultery, incest or rape. All are created in the image of God, are fully human and possess the same dignity and value as

anyone else. That God infuses a rational soul when
human biological materials are arranged in a certain
manner in no way implies that God approves the way in
which certain conceptions come about.

It has been suggested by some Catholics that human
clones might not have human souls because of their asexual
origin. This position is contrary to Church teaching for a
number of reasons. Firstly, a human being simply cannot
have anything other than a human soul. A human soul is the
only soul that can animate a human body. A human being
without a human soul is not a human being. But clones are
human beings, with the genome and developmental powers
of human beings. Secondly, the logic which says that an
asexually produced human does not or might not possess a
human soul must also say that human embryos produced by
twinning (i.e. splitting of a prior embryo either naturally or
artificially) lack such souls. It would clearly be absurd to
say that twins lack souls, simply because they come to be
(in most cases, by a natural accident) in an asexual way.

Nonsexual reproduction[4]

The Church's teaching regarding the status of the embryo
casts light on the Church's position with regard to IVF

---

[4] Nonsexual reproduction refers to reproduction achieved otherwise than
through the sexual act between man and woman. Asexual reproduction
refers to reproduction achieved without fertilisation - i.e. the
combination of a male and female gamete.

and cloning. The usual practice of IVF involves obtaining several mature ova from a woman whose ovaries have been chemically stimulated in such a way as to produce them. The ova are removed from her and placed in a dish in the laboratory (*in vitro*). Sperm (usually obtained via masturbation) is then prepared and placed with the ova in the dish, where fertilisation takes place. After cultivation, a number of embryos are selected and transferred to the uterus. 'Spare' embryos are frozen for later implantation; destroyed; or fatally experimented upon. Embryos are sometimes deliberately created for research purposes.

On the question of IVF embryos, *Donum Vitae* states: "Human embryos obtained in vitro are human beings and subjects with rights: their dignity and right to life must be respected from the first moment of their existence. It is immoral to produce human embryos destined to be exploited as disposable 'biological material' [I.5]". What is true of IVF embryos is equally true of clone embryos. *Evangelium Vitae* in condemning embryo experimentation states: "This moral condemnation also regards the procedures that exploit living human embryos and foetuses - sometimes 'produced' for this purpose by *in vitro* fertilisation - either used as 'biological material' or as providers of organs or tissue for transplants in the treatment of certain diseases. The killing of innocent human creatures, even if carried out to help others, constitutes an absolutely unacceptable act [63]".

The Church thus makes clear that respect for human persons prohibits certain kinds of choice in relation to them, be they embryos or older human beings. However, it is not only damaging actions carried out on IVF embryos that the Church condemns. As *Donum Vitae* states: "Fertilisation achieved outside the bodies of the couple remains by this very fact deprived of the meanings and values which are expressed in the language of the body and in the union of human persons... In reality, the origin of a human person is the result of an act of giving. The one conceived must be the fruit of his parents' love. He cannot be desired or conceived as the product of an intervention of medical or biological techniques; that would be equivalent to reducing him to an object of scientific technology." [II.4].

The next section will look at the Church's teaching on the meaning of sex within marriage. Here it should be noted that the Church regards the very process of IVF (and cloning) as wrong because unjust to the early human being. To generate a human being via IVF or cloning is to engage in a production process. Necessarily, the relation between product and maker is one of radical inequality. "Producing" a child places the parent in a position of domination over that child. Regardless of the motives of the parents of an IVF embryo, to choose to put oneself in this position is to choose an initial relationship with a child contrary to the idea of a family as a communion of persons possessing equal dignity. To choose to have a child by cloning is an even greater insult to the dignity of the child, because here the reproduction is asexual, and dominance extends to the genome of the child.

Therefore it should be clear that the basic reason why the Church regards nonsexual and asexual reproduction as wrong is not so much that they involve artificial techniques, but that they deny the dignity of the human person so created.

The link between creating embryos as though they were mere products, and then treating them as such, was directly addressed by Pope John Paul II when speaking to the 18th International Congress of the Transplantation Society on August 30th 2000:

"In any event methods that fail to respect the dignity and value of the person must always be avoided. I am thinking in particular of attempts at human cloning with a view to obtaining organs for transplants: these techniques, insofar as they involve the manipulation and destruction of human embryos, are not morally acceptable, even when their proposed end is good in itself."

Already at the time of *Donum Vitae*, the Church was speaking out against procedures which had arisen, or might arise, in the wake of IVF. *Donum Vitae* condemns: "...attempts or plans for fertilisation between human and animal gametes and the gestation of human embryos in the uterus of animals... *These procedures are contrary to the human dignity proper to the embryo...*" [I.6]

While it is often unclear in the first case whether a human embryo has actually come into being from such techniques, the procedure itself shows no respect for that possibility, and thus treats any human being arising from the procedure as a product. Extrapolating from this, and for the same reasons, the transfer of human nuclei into animal ova is incompatible with a respect for human dignity. The aim of creating a clone human being via a form of human-animal transgenesis is worthy of condemnation in similar ways to cloning using a human ovum. In one respect it could be worse insofar as it further offends against human dignity because it may cause a human being to be formed from an animal gamete. Even to risk the possibility that a human being may be produced by such a procedure is to show a complete lack of respect for human dignity.

Sex and marriage

Although the dignity of the embryo and the genuine respect it deserves form the primary reason for condemning certain methods of reproduction, there are further important and related reasons why the Church condemns such methods. These reasons can only be understood in the light of the Church's teaching on marriage and the meaning of the conjugal act.

The Church has made clear throughout the ages that the vocation to marriage is written in the very nature of man and woman as they come from the hand of the Creator.

Scripture records Christ's words, recalling Genesis: "Have you not read that He who made them from the beginning made them male and female and said, "For this reason a man shall leave his father and mother and be joined to his wife, and the two shall become one flesh'? So they are no longer two, but one flesh." [*Matthew* 19:4-7; see also *Mark* 10:4-12]. St Paul, continuing this teaching, stresses the unique mystery of marriage, and the way in which spouses are called to reflect the love and devotion which Christ the Bridegroom has for the Church His Bride, and through which the Church loves and serves Him in return. [*Ephesians* Ch 5]

The sacrament of marriage involves two people, a man and a woman, declaring in the presence of God that they are establishing an objective state, a covenant with Him and each other, in which, as spouses, they become gifts for one another, subordinated to one another under Christ. In sexual intercourse both embrace and receive each other from the hands of God their Maker.

Marriage therefore is not an arbitrary contractual arrangement but an institution established by Christ. In sexual union, this theological understanding of marriage is fully realised where the personal conjugal act of husband and wife intimately co-operates with the creative act of God. Sexual congress between husband and wife takes place when Divine action and procreative union of man and woman meet. A child is the ultimate fruit of that meeting.

Marriage creates an indissoluble commitment between a man and a woman, which fosters a special personal commitment: a commitment of self-giving love, with each spouse recognising the uniqueness and preciousness of the other. Marriage vows demand not only a fundamental commitment to one's spouse but also a loving openness to the creation of new life. The full meaning of marriage reaches beyond itself to bring a new, unique, unrepeatable and precious human life into being. This uniquely creative enterprise honours a child's dignity in that it is for his/her good that a husband and wife are committed unconditionally in acceptance of each other. A child conceived as the fruit of sexual intercourse expressive of unconditional love is a child whose dignity and equality have been fully respected. Anything less than this is lacking in respect for the dignity of the child.

As the *Catechism* states: "A child is not something *owed* to one, but is a *gift*. The 'supreme gift of marriage' is a human person. A child may not be considered a piece of property, an idea to which an alleged "right to a child" would lead. In this area, only the child possesses genuine rights: the right 'to be the fruit of the specific act of the conjugal love of his parents' and 'the right to be respected from the moment of his conception.'". [2378]

The Church holds that "marriage and married love are by nature ordered to the procreation and education of children" (*Gaudium et Spes* 50). The unique nature of marital intercourse involves the mutual gift of complementary procreativity. It is this that makes true conjugal acts unitive of spouses. For this reason the encyclical *Humanae Vitae*, reiterating the constant teaching of the Church, stated that there is: "...an inseparable connection, established by God, which man on his own initiative may not break, between the unitive significance and the procreative significance which are both inherent to the marriage act." [12].

Contraception, IVF and human cloning all involve a deliberate separation of these two elements of the conjugal act, and thus subvert its inherent meaning of total self-giving. The Church categorically condemns all three. *Donum Vitae* says of the latter two: "These procedures are contrary to the human dignity proper to the embryo, and at the same time they are contrary to the right of every person to be conceived and to be born within marriage and from marriage. Also, attempts or hypotheses for obtaining a human being without any connection with sexuality through "twin fission", cloning or parthenogenesis are to be considered contrary to the moral law, since they are in opposition to the dignity *both* of human procreation and of the conjugal union." [[I.6] my emphasis].

In emphasising the importance of conjugal communion the Church recognises that it is the foundation for the broader communion of the family, of parents and children, brothers and sisters with each other, of relatives and the wider household community. In *Familiaris Consortio* (Regarding the role of the Christian family in the modern world) [1981] Pope John Paul II states: "This communion is rooted in the natural bonds of flesh and blood, and grows to its specifically human perfection with the establishment and maturing of the still deeper and richer bonds of the spirit: the love that animates the interpersonal relationships of the different members of the family constitutes the interior strength that shapes family life and communion" [21].

The Church is therefore absolutely opposed to all ways of conceiving children which distort the natural and spiritual bonds of family members with each other. It recognises that the fundamental and intense human form of community found in the covenant of marriage, when characterised by genuine self-giving love, begins to reflect the Trinitarian life of God, that unity in community that is a communion of self-giving love.

We could not begin to understand that Trinitarian life if God had not given us sex and family relations. The very terms of the Trinity, that is, the very nature of God Himself, can only begin to be understood in a world where family relations exist. Insofar as a society deliberately undermines and perverts that unity in communion present in family relations it cuts itself off from knowing its Creator.

EXAMINING THE ARGUMENTS

Arguments about human cloning take place in a societal framework where many have no religious views whatsoever. It is important to show that the Church's position on human cloning is defensible on grounds that people of other faiths or no faith can appreciate. That is what this chapter aims to do.

Cloning for birth

Human experimentation

In discussing live-birth cloning in the first chapter some practical dangers were pointed out. The risks live-birth cloning would impose on human beings are so grave as to constitute overriding reasons for forbidding it. Human subjects would have to be experimented upon in order for live-birth cloning to become a reality. Those experimented upon would be women who donate or sell eggs, gestational mothers, and children-to-be. Ethical codes and regulations governing human experimentation were formulated in the wake of the atrocities of World War II, and have become widely accepted. These codes include the Nuremberg Code of 1947 and the subsequent Declaration of Helsinki of 1964 (since updated). Principle 5 of the Nuremberg Code dictates that: "No experiment should be conducted where there is an *a priori* reason to believe that death or disabling injury will occur". Principle 7 of the same Code enjoins that: "Proper preparations should be made and adequate facilities provided to protect the experimental subject against even remote possibilities of injury, disability or death". Both the Code and the Declaration absolutely forbid non-therapeutic and harmful procedures carried out on non-consenting human subjects, regardless of any supposed societal benefits. Underlying these codes is the principle that all human beings possess equal dignity and certain inviolable rights.

The codes recognise that in considering ethical problems arising from human experimentation, the welfare and safety of the human research subject must be paramount. The ethical values of the relationship between doctor and subject must take priority over any research or commercial interests. The safety of children-to-be, egg donors and gestational mothers with regard to live-birth cloning should be considered in this context.

The practical risks to the child-to-be and the gestational mother have already been outlined, but are worth revisiting. Animal experimentation has shown that the vast majority of clones die pre-implantation, or are implanted and then die. Of the very few that survive to birth, a large proportion have died soon after, or have developed non-fatal abnormalities. With cloning by somatic nuclear transfer it has been suggested that the

DNA of the transferred nucleus will contain modifications accumulated over the time before it was transferred. The nucleus, on its 'second run', may make the new clone individual more prone to disease and disability because of these earlier modifications. The risks to the gestational mother are both physically and psychologically grave. In one animal cloning experiment nearly a third of cattle pregnant with clones died in late pregnancy. Miscarriages of clones are far more frequent than those following natural pregnancy. Women who choose to donate eggs are also at risk, insofar as their future health could be affected by the treatments used for the retrieval of eggs, and the drugs used for **superovulation**.

In order to make human cloning 'safe', experiments upon human subjects would be required. Primarily, those experiments would be on human subjects who could not consent. Even if the animal cloning data did not reveal the grave risks to which humans would be exposed, so much remains unknown of species-specific differences that it is difficult to see how human experimentation in this area could ever be justified.

Two pro-cloning objections

Some cloning advocates have argued that it is acceptable to clone human beings because the harm caused to a clone individual becomes morally irrelevant if it is an unavoidable part of bringing that individual into existence. They insist that such procedures are justified provided the clone individual's life is 'worth living'. They further insist that it is absurd to demand consent from an individual whose coming into existence depends on the procedures they propose.

Both of these arguments fail. To see why the first argument fails, consider the following example. Imagine a future genetic engineer who, in the very process of producing a human embryo, manipulates its genome. This manipulation is necessary to produce the damaged embryo he intends to create. His aim is to ensure that that human individual, far from being healthy, will, when he grows up, be blind, deaf, and unable to speak. The genetic engineer is so keen to achieve his malicious goal that he will not create a healthy embryo although it would be in his power to do so. According to the pro-cloning argument, the human individual may still lead a worthwhile life, which he otherwise would not, and therefore such procedures could be justified because the harm they cause is 'morally irrelevant'! Giving existence to a human being gives no one the right to harm or degrade that human being in the process of bringing him into existence.

The second argument simply misses the point. The fact that one cannot get consent from the subject does not make the getting of that consent irrelevant. If an experimenter ought not to perform an experiment without consent, then he ought not to do this. This is recognised by the Nuremburg and Helsinki declarations, both of which emphasise the importance of consent because of the protection it offers for the weak and vulnerable in relation to those who are powerful.

Donor problems

In order for large-scale experimentation to take place, a large supply of ova will be required. Animal experiments suggest that the number of eggs required to produce even one live-born clone would be enormous. In order to obtain the amount of eggs needed it is very likely that financial incentives will be offered to women, thus changing the meaning of the term 'egg donor'. The scope for exploitation of poor women is very large, especially given the known health risks that attach to superovulation. In the absence of women willing to donate their eggs, it has been proposed that eggs from aborted female foetuses could be used. The reduction of these babies to mere means for the end of cloning would represent a further step in the degradation of human life.

On top of these extrinsic and practical reasons for rejecting live-birth cloning, there are serious intrinsic reasons for rejecting it. Whereas the above objections to live-birth cloning are based on issues of safety and consent and relate to individuals, intrinsic reasons against live-birth cloning provide us with arguments as to why cloning is wrong *in itself*. One might imagine a day when techniques for live-birth cloning were perfected (at the cost of many dead babies, disabled children and distraught mothers). It is therefore necessary to give reasons against the practice itself.

Moral intuition

Before approaching these reasons, it should be noted that many people find the very idea of live-birth cloning repugnant. This reaction might be characterised as a pre-theoretical feeling or intuition relating to any of the various aspects of human cloning. This repugnance suggests to people that what is being proposed with regard to live-birth cloning is something very wrong. It is quite possible to *know* that something is morally wrong without being able to articulate exactly *why* and for what reasons it is wrong. Leon Kass, the Jewish ethicist, has spoken in this context of the 'wisdom of repugnance', and has characterised this as 'an emotional expression of deep wisdom, beyond reason's power to fully articulate it.' It is certainly true that many people regard practices such as incest as morally abhorrent, without being able to articulate cogent reasons that capture the precise nature of the wrong committed. The wrongness of incest is not adequately accounted for by pointing out that it poses genetic risks to children conceived as a result of it. This does not mean that incest's wrongness is not wrongness *for reasons*, merely that it may be difficult to articulate these reasons.

Human cloning, like incest, challenges fundamental values. It directly confronts the common human understanding of procreation, the purposes of sexual differentiation and complementarity, and respect for life. As these values are so fundamental, it is perhaps appropriate that revulsion acts as a warning when they appear to be threatened. Nevertheless, it can always be asked whether a given feeling of repugnance is reasonable, or at least partially based on good reasons.

Procreation

The most obvious threat posed by somatic cell nuclear transfer cloning is to the nature of human procreation and the rearing of children. Cloning, as a form of asexual reproduction, completely displaces the procreative act between a man and a woman. As human beings we are bodily beings. Our living bodies are intrinsic to our unified personal experience. Sexual procreation between a man and a woman is a single act performed by a pair. In this regard the man and woman form, in the words of philosopher Germain Grisez, a single reproductive (or procreative) principle. It is because as persons we are a dynamic unity of body and soul that our bodily acts carry an inherent meaning. In light of the couple forming a single reproductive principle, we can see that an organic unity of persons is present in the procreative type of act. The meaning of these acts is therefore not absolutely reducible to the personal projects of the couple. These acts have an inherent connection to the good of the transmission of life. To deny this and to claim that the meaning of sexual union is determined simply by the desire/will of the couple, is to deny the basic purpose of sexual union between a man and a woman, and with it the normative meanings of our sexual differentiation and complementarity.

By giving themselves in love to each other and bringing together their gametes (sperm and ovum) through a personal sexual act, the couple each give genes to form a completely new human individual. The new human is genetically unique, related to the parents but distinct from them. He has come to be as a result of the procreative act of his parents and his genetic make-up is unpredictable. He is genetically linked to the past, yet open to the future. These features carry the valuable message that the child is the gift and fruit of sexual procreation, who, as such, must be unconditionally accepted in all his contingent and unplanned characteristics. He is not produced or chosen as a *particular* child with *particular* features according to a *particular* template. He is not custom-made according to the will of his parents. The fact that the child is a unique and contingent gift, the result of sexual union, invites acceptance of a different yet equal and related person, not someone the parents own, or who exists only for their own purposes. The sense that a child is not a possession is an important one for parents to have, lest they be tempted to treat him as if he were. In rearing a child the parents should guide and to some extent mould the child, but only so that he or she may develop a truly separate identity from them.

Production

The clone child will not come to be as the result of a sexual act between two persons, but will be *produced* in a laboratory following a series of separate acts. These acts will include the extracting of an adult cell, the extracting of a woman's ovum and removal of its nucleus, the technical procedure of fusing the cell with the enucleated ovum *in vitro*, the transferral of the early embryo to a woman's womb. At no point could there be said to be, in any of these acts, an organic unity of persons. Each act is part of a production process. The child is brought into being according to set criteria, in this case with a pre-selected genetic pattern. Thus the 'parents' of the clone have, or aim at having, complete control over what *type* of child they are to have in the same way a producer has complete control over a product. A child produced by such methods is thus reduced to the status of an object of the producers' will. This inequality of relation, whereby producers wilfully place themselves in a position of dominion over the product, is radically opposed both to the meaning of procreative acts and to the equality and dignity of the child. Such a choice is therefore intrinsically wrong. Putting oneself in the position of producer greatly increases the temptation to value one's child according to how he/she measures up to one's requirements.

Some advocates of cloning say, in response to this point, that IVF and **artificial insemination** are widely practised and that they too involve a production process. What makes cloning so different? It is true that IVF and artificial insemination involve a production process. But if the technical production of children in this way is inherently wrong, then this merely demonstrates that cloning can be classified, along with IVF and artificial insemination, as inherently wrong for this reason. The fact that a child produced by IVF or artificial insemination can be lovingly accepted into a family does nothing to show that the production process used to create that child is not fundamentally immoral.

However, cloning does introduce new problems. With IVF, while we have a production process, we are still dealing with the union of sperm and ova, albeit in a petri dish. The IVF child will still be genetically different from but related to its father and mother. A clone is asexually created, will be a late genetic replica of the adult cell donor, will be only partially related to the ovum donor and will have no father at all. The clone child will have been custom-made to a genetic blueprint in the way that an IVF child is not[5]. The extent of dominion exercised by the parents over the child is therefore greater in the case of cloning.

Identity

The clone child, while being a near genetic replica of the **adult cell donor**, will be an entirely separate individual. We are not reducible, as human persons, to our genes. Human identical twins occurring in nature are closer to each other genetically than a clone and its adult cell donor would be, but remain completely separate persons and undergo separate experiences. Radical similarities between persons do not make them identical as persons. One can only talk of similarity against a background of difference.

But the point is not that a clone would not be a distinct person from his/her adult cell donor. It is rather that he/she will have been *deliberately* produced as a replica of another human, and thus will *appear* to be a replacement copy of someone, and not a unique original. To attempt to replicate someone genetically is to attempt something that radically removes genetic differences between people. Such differences certainly symbolise the uniqueness and separateness of persons, and protect us against the idea of treating people as replaceable. Cloning, which makes mass replication possible, would

---

[5] Although in very many cases the IVF child will have been selected, for particular features, from a group of IVF embryos.

undermine this important symbolism and thereby handicap the formation of a sense of individual identity.

Our *genetic* uniqueness helps us to have a sense of our *essential* uniqueness, and carries with it the message that we have the possibility of living a life that is fully our own. The clone is denied this option insofar as he is, genetically, re-enacting another's life. The clone's possibility of self-determination, a value our present society claims to respect, would be undermined given that he could always be compared to the one from whom he was formed. In many cases he will have been formed precisely in order to resemble an original. He will live life in the shadow of his original whose actual development could be used as a template in the clone's rearing.

Even if the clone were never to meet his or her original, the very awareness of such a person's existence would lead to a sense of living in the shadow of this unknown person. To argue, as some advocates of cloning do, that it is best to keep the clone in ignorance of how he came to be, is implicitly to admit the existence of the very problem that those who oppose cloning have pointed out.

Some of those who favour cloning have argued that it could be a way for parents to 'replace' previous children that have died. Here the child would be deliberately deprived of a living genetic parent, and explicitly seen as something other than irreplaceable and unique in him or herself. Others propose cloning famous people - for example, brilliant scientists. Such examples serve to clarify the radical nature of the attack on personal identity that cloning would allow for.

Identical twins

Naturally occurring identical twins[6], unlike clones, are born together and are not produced by an act of manufacture. They are not planned and therefore cannot be made in order to replicate another. They are immune to the problems of measuring up to an elder twin, or gaining knowledge of how certain genetic traits will play out. An identical twin will be as unaware as anyone else of how he or his twin will develop genetically. There can be no perception of an older genetic template with an already tested potential to undermine the sense of the uniqueness of the self.

It must be added that there is strong evidence that even naturally occurring identical twins can encounter identity problems in their social development, particularly when, for example, parents are reluctant for the twins to develop separate identities. Cloning will, in many cases, be performed precisely so that a particular original will be replicated, and for no other reason than that. An intention to undermine a separate identity could be expressed by the very act of cloning.

---

[6] Identical twins will be even more similar to each other than a clone and its original in that they will share the same mitochondrial DNA and will have grown in the same womb.

Motherhood and identity

The formation of a sense of identity is deeply influenced by familial relations. The clone has no father as such. A single woman could take an adult cell from herself and have it fused with one of her enucleated eggs thereby producing a clone of herself who will be even closer to her genetically than a clone who is not made using her ovum. She will then be the belated genetic twin-sister, as well as the birth mother, of the clone child. How, one may ask in a case such as this, is the child to develop any sort of self-identity? The choices made by the single woman will deliberately deprive the clone child of both a genetic and a social father, thereby distorting that child's relations with the male sex.

In another case a clone could come to be with a partial genetic mother (whose enucleated ovum is fused with an adult donor cell to create the clone embryo), a gestational mother (in whose uterus the clone will be implanted and brought to birth) and a commissioning mother (who ordered the clone). Are these separate people to be regarded as quasi-parents, and what duties do they have to the clone child they helped to bring about? Which one is duty bound, for the sake of the child, to take on the role of social mother? The genetic mother is not a genetic mother in the ordinary sense, in that she will not have contributed a haploid set of chromosomes to the baby, but will only have provided an enucleated ovum, thereby contributing only mitochondrial genes (see chapter 1). The gestational mother will, again, be only a partial mother to a child that is not fully her own and in whose creation she played no part. The commissioning 'mother' may become the social mother, but has no prior claim which could trump that of the woman who gives birth.

The distancing of the gestational mother from the partial genetic mother of the child in the case of cloning shows up the radical fragmentation and limitation of maternity, not to mention the obliteration of paternity. What would be the duties of the adult cell donor toward his/her younger genetic twin? These questions arise, at least in part, because the clone has been denied real parents. If the 'genetic mother' providing the ovum is also the gestational mother, we still have a case of partial surrogacy, because the ovum provider's genetic contribution is absolutely minimal. She carries a child who is almost entirely formed by the genetic contribution of another. In the case of a donated egg being fused with an adult donor cell following which the clone is implanted into another woman to gestate, a further gap is introduced, a further confusion as to who the mother is. All of these factors serve to remove from the child those traditional ties to parents which can act as a protection against his or her maltreatment. This situation, coupled with the inherent meaning of the production process that has been used to create the clone, leave the clone vulnerable to many types of abuse.

Dignity of women

As well as being unjust to the clone, such procedures attack the dignity of women. The division of maternity ensures that childbearing loses its proper origin in an act of self-giving conjugal love. The separation of women's fertility from the unitive and generative meaning of the conjugal act distorts a woman's relation to her fertility even more than in the case of IVF. Aside from the already mentioned physical dangers that women gestating clones would experience, the deliberate separation of a woman's fertility from procreative conjugal acts is undermining of her sense of the dynamic unity of the person that she is. The idea that bearing children is only contingently connected with sex further distances both men and women from the good at which sex primarily aims: the good of the transmission of life. In cloning, the woman becomes the incubator, the male or female cell donor a hireling who need have no tie to the birth mother, and the child the product of a manufacturing process.

Familial relations

One might say that the woman who gestates and gives birth to the child should be called the 'mother' of the child, and this may well be socially desirable. In an ideal case, a clone child would be welcomed into this woman's family. But the familial relations that the clone child will come into will be confused and unclear.

Cloning does much more than undermine natural biological connections. Adoption, after all, bypasses biological connections and, though not an ideal response to the needs of children, allows many to live happy lives in loving families. Consider the case where a parent of the egg donor contributed an adult cell, and the donor gave birth to a clone of her own mother. Or imagine a case of a mother bearing a clone of her own grandfather. The sense of generations in a family such as this would be so grossly distorted that it is unclear whether the relationships forming such a unit should be called a family. The increased probability of incestuous relationships between, say, a mother and a clone from her husband's cell would be a real danger. This is because the clone may well strongly resemble a younger version of the father as he grows up.

Clone children, like adopted children or those conceived with donor gametes, will have a perfectly reasonable desire to find out their genetic heritage. In the case of the clone there will be a desire to discover and meet one's genetic older twin, assuming that one is being raised outside this person's family. Human experience gives the lie to the belief that genetic inheritance is absolutely irrelevant, and that social parentage is all that matters. At present there are men and women who 'donate' sperm or ova for the creation of children they ensure will never have any social connection with them.

This has already become big business, with desirable males/females being able to charge extra for their gametes to be used. 'Donor' offspring are thus robbed of their rightful inheritance in terms of parental care. Cloning, as well as degrading the clone, will simply exacerbate this iniquitous situation, further entrenching the idea that one generation can prosper at the expense of the next.

Cloning as fertility treatment

Some advocates of cloning for birth claim that it should be seen as a medical treatment. After all, it is one way in which an infertile couple might be able to have children. It might, as we have seen, allow an infertile man or woman who could not be treated in existing ways to have a child to whom he/she would be genetically related.

The overall aim of medicine is the restoration and maintenance of healthy functioning. Infertility is a type of dysfunction and it is medicine's aim to try and restore a couple's reproductive health. Cloning, its advocates claim, will allow the infertile couple to have children to whom they have a genetic connection. But how will cloning help treat infertility in this situation? It certainly will not restore a natural function, for there is no natural function giving one "the ability to have a late genetic replica of myself". Cloning will merely be a way of satisfying the desires of infertile couples. But whether those desires are reasonable or moral is all-important. The desire to have a clone child generates no 'right' to have one. The medical profession is not merely a tool for enabling patients to pursue their desires. The goods that medicine pursues are ordered by the structure of the human body, not by whatever a patient happens to want. If medicine was simply a tool that patients could use to pursue their projects (in this case parental projects) it would be difficult to see how we could judge what a moral practice of medicine could be.

Infertility can be a distressing condition for couples. Cloning is likely to be offered to infertile couples who can't be 'treated' by other means. But it is no part of medicine to give patients whatever they want, by whatever means, however harmful or demeaning. This is so especially when acceptable alternatives, such as adoption, are available.

Worries about eugenics

One way couples attempt to treat infertility is by IVF. At present many IVF embryos are genetically screened. If they are found to have a genetic disorder they are destroyed. They are destroyed in the name of 'quality-control': a term which used to be applied only to the sub-human. These embryos are treated as products of a manufacturing process. They are not unconditionally accepted. Eugenic selection of this sort has become commonplace and is expanding. IVF is now being used so that couples can, destructively, select the sex of their child.

By permitting cloning, with its radical form of parental control, it becomes difficult to see how the next stage of eugenic parental control could be argued against. The prospect of radically altering (rather than copying) the child's DNA is that next stage. Such a process could be extended to such a degree that the very nature of the organism created would be blurred. The boundary between human and non-human would become questionable. The extent of the power that one generation would have over the next would have no parallel in human history. Some scientists have openly declared that cloning is but one step toward 'perfecting' and 'directing' reproduction in such a way that future generations will be 'genetically enhanced'. Philosopher and cloning advocate Gregory Pence has talked of 'superior children' being produced via cloning. The hope of some is that the contingent and unpredictable element in human reproduction (which carries a valuable message about the child's uniqueness) will be abolished. If clones can receive traits from desirable originals, why not tamper with the genome for further benefits? Already an advocate of cloning, scientist Lee M. Silver, has talked of a two-tier society, consisting of the "Gen Rich" (gene rich) who will be able to genetically enrich their children, and "Naturals" who will be denied this opportunity. Once cloning establishes the principle that parents can have total control over a child's genome, it is difficult to see how one could argue against full-scale genetic engineering. If positive genetic 'enhancement' of human beings becomes a goal, we will have moved beyond the idea of medicine as restorative of healthy functioning, and into a world where detached and free-floating ideas of excellence will be used to adjudge the acceptability of interference. When notions of the good in relation to health have no grounding other than in the desires of those with power, their arbitrariness should, at the very least, give us pause for reflection over genetic engineering.[7]

Societal effects

A society that allows live-birth cloning is a society profoundly different from one that does not. The former, by openly accepting such a practice, is complicit in it. It is a society that thinks children may be deprived of a mother and father, and that 'parental' control over children should be so absolute that even a child's genome ought to be fully subject to it. It is a society that is prepared to replace the idea of children as unconditional gifts whose dignity demands respect, with the idea that children are products, acceptable in so far as they fit in with parental projects. Some may argue that this is the society we live in today, and that cloning is merely an extension of the values of such a society. Asexual conception, however, is a radical step beyond all that has

---

[7] See Helen Watt's booklet *Gene Therapy* in this series.

gone before. Can we seriously talk of the common good
when whole categories of persons will have had their
very identity undermined, and their place in a framework
of equality and unconditional acceptance deliberately
taken from them? Can we talk of the common good when
a whole class of persons will be visible as 'copies' of
originals - whose very faces may be advertisements for
the way in which their owners were conceived? The right
to genetic privacy will simply not exist for these people.

Only societies already corrupt in their attitude to children
and procreation could even conceive of human cloning as
morally acceptable. Such attitudes, and the reproductive
technologies arising from them, should be questioned by
everyone who cares about the society in which they live.

Embryo splitting

Some have suggested that cloning by embryo splitting is
more morally acceptable than cloning by somatic cell
nuclear transfer, because it mimics what happens in
nature. Lee M. Silver has argued that we have no 'right'
not to be clones, given that nature grants no such 'right'
to identical twins. But the domain of natural processes is
not the moral domain, which is concerned with human
actions. The fact that something occurs naturally does
nothing to provide us with a reason for doing it
intentionally. Earthquakes occur 'naturally', but that does
not give us a reason to intentionally engineer one.

On top of this, there is evidence to suggest that naturally occurring identical twinning is not so much the consequence of healthy functioning, but rather the result of some reproductive dysfunction. Identical twins are far more at risk from disease and early death than are singletons.

Cloning for birth by embryo splitting would not produce the generational problems discussed above. Nor would it produce the same kind of identity-undermining features as would somatic nuclear transfer cloning. However, embryo splitting raises other ethical problems.

Identical twinning occurs in nature in one of two ways. One way is that at an early stage of embryonic development, a symmetric split occurs in the embryo, resulting in two embryos developing. This means that the original embryo dies, and two identical ones are produced. The other way in which identical twinning may occur is that the original human embryo splits asymmetrically and thus continues when a newly formed twin begins. Deliberate embryo splitting, if done in a symmetrical way, would involve killing the original embryo in order to produce two new embryos. If not done in a symmetrical way, it is theoretically possible that the original embryo could survive a splitting procedure and a twin be produced asexually. Here no killing would be involved in the splitting, but the survival of the original and the new embryo would be severely compromised by such a procedure. In practice,

the vast majority of embryos created have been
destroyed when embryo splitting has been attempted.
The practice of deliberately splitting embryos is further
evidence of how the embryo is viewed as a product when
it is non-sexually conceived.

Cloning for research/transplantation

Debate over the destructive use of embryos for research
purposes is not new. Following the advent of IVF, the
Warnock Committee in the UK recommended in 1984
that destructive research on early human embryos be
allowed for specific projects. Research on human
embryos aged up to 14 days is permitted under the
Human Fertilisation and Embryology Act of 1990.
Embryos used in research may be either 'spare' embryos
created for infertile couples or embryos expressly created
for destructive research purposes. Destructive research on
clone and IVF embryos has more recently been legalised
in order to find treatments for those with certain illnesses
and disabilities (see chapter 1 on embryonic stem cells).
Many people who are adamantly opposed to cloning for
birth believe that cloning for research/transplantation is
acceptable. Is this position morally tenable?

Status of the embryo

The question at the root of destructive embryo research is
- 'Should human embryos be regarded as moral subjects?'

The answer to this question will determine whether the proposed research is morally acceptable or not. If a society regards the deliberate killing of innocent human beings as fundamentally immoral, then, if it regards human embryos as human beings, it must regard their deliberate destruction as fundamentally immoral.

A new human individual emerges at the moment of conception. Sperm and ova are not individuals, but cells belonging, respectively, to the father and mother of the individual to be formed. This new individual cannot be identified with either parent. Standard embryology textbooks state that the beginning of a new member of the human species occurs when a zygote is produced from the fusion of sperm and ovum. A zygote can also be produced asexually, either by twinning or by cloning. However, in neither case does this change the truth that at the moment of conception, achieved either sexually or asexually, a new individual has begun with specific developmental powers. This new one-cell human embryo has the potential to actively organise and develop him or herself to further stages of human maturity. The potential to mature into an older human being is only possible if the organism is *already* a human being. He/she will remain the same self-integrating organism throughout his/her life. You and I were once single-cell zygotes; we were never once a sperm or an egg.

Functionalism

To deny that a human organism is a person is to deny that we, as persons, are essentially human physical organisms. The terms 'person' and 'human being' are not equivalent. Rational aliens, for example, would be persons but not human beings. However, human beings are a subset of the category persons. We do not happen to possess a physical organism. We *are* rational physical organisms. We come to be when the integrated and self-directing physical organisms we are come to be. To define personhood functionally, which is to say only in terms of certain exhibited behaviour, is to ignore the distinction between being a person and functioning as a person. It is impossible to function as a person without being one. However, a human person may, at certain times of life, lack certain functional abilities that humans usually have, while still remaining a person. A person in a coma is still a person, although his specifically human function of thought may not be active at the present time. An infant is still a person, although he may lack certain specifically human functions through immaturity. The same is true of an embryo.

Value of persons

Persons are intrinsically valuable in themselves simply in virtue of being persons. If this was not the case, and the value of persons was dependent on their functional abilities, we would be committed to the view that the value of persons would increase/decrease proportionately to the development of their functions. But this would mean that babies, young children, the sick, the elderly, could reasonably be regarded as lacking in or having no value. Valuation on such a basis is inherently subjective and relative to the interests of the valuer. The notion of human rights makes no sense unless based upon the idea that each of us has value in virtue of what we *are*.

We are, of course, more than just physical organisms. But to identify the term human being with human person is not to deny this. On the contrary, it is to recognise that a living human being cannot have a sub-personal status. It is to recognise that a living human body simply cannot exist without a 'life-principle' or soul.

The embryo, because it is so small, may not have the powerful emotional appeal of a baby. But it is merely a younger version of the latter. To deliberately kill/destroy a human embryo is to kill/destroy a human being whose life is intrinsically valuable. As this life is intrinsically valuable, it is so at all its stages. Therefore killing/destroying an embryo is as serious as destroying a baby, child or adult. A human embryo has the same absolute right not to be destroyed or non-therapeutically invaded as any innocent older human being.

Five opposing arguments

The following argument has been made: persons must have brains; early embryos do not have brains; therefore early embryos are not persons. This argument misses the point that the early embryo has the capacity to develop a brain in the same way a baby has the capacity to develop and learn a language. But just as the baby is no less a human before it has exercised this capacity, so too with the embryo. Moreover, one cannot grow a human brain without being a human, and one cannot be a human without being a person.

Another argument used to justify destructive experimentation on embryos is the fact that in nature large numbers of seemingly viable human embryos that have come to be through normal conception fail to implant in the mother's womb and perish. There is much dispute over the numbers that actually perish, and whether those that perish are properly formed human embryos, rather than the results of incomplete conceptions. Leaving this aside, the argument does nothing to justify destructive experimentation on embryos. Nature is not a moral agent. Consider that today infant mortality rates are far higher in Africa than in Europe. Does it follow from this that we should be allowed to kill African infants because many are likely to die soon? Does the higher infant mortality rate make it reasonable to suggest that African infants aren't fully human?

Some try to argue that only when the embryo implants in the mother's womb should it be regarded as having significant moral status. It follows, on this argument, that pre-implantation human embryos created via IVF or cloning have lesser moral status than embryos who have been implanted. The argument assumes that the embryo only acquires its potential to become an individual human organism on implantation in the mother's womb. But the human embryo, as we have seen, is an *actual* human individual at conception - with the potential to develop into a more mature human individual. The fact that an embryo outside its natural place in its mother's womb will, if not implanted, only have the ability to realise some of its natural capacities does nothing to change either its inherent powers or its moral status. It merely shows that the embryo has been deprived of the possibility of flourishing in its natural environment.

Some argue that because 'spare' IVF embryos will be destroyed anyway, we are justified in destructively experimenting on them. The reasoning here is, again, quite unsound. Prisoners on Death Row are going to be executed, but it would be absurd to suggest that we therefore are justified in conducting harmful experiments on them. We ourselves will die one day, but does this fact have a bearing on our right not to be destroyed or harmed?

Finally, some argue that an early embryo is just a cell or cluster of cells, and has the same status as any human cell. Such a position ignores the fact that the zygote is an integrated and self-developing whole, whereas an ordinary human cell is not. The early embryo is an actual human organism with developmental potential to become a foetus, baby, child and adult. A human cell is merely part of an organism and has no such human developmental powers: the most it has is a passive potential to contribute (as in cloning) to the formation of a new human organism. Gametes, as opposed to body cells, have an active potential to contribute to forming an embryo; however, they themselves have no developmental powers and do not survive the process of conception.

Societal effects

To clone human beings for the specific purpose of using them in destructive research can never be compatible with the respect that the status of the human embryo demands.

From 1990 onwards it has been legally permissible in Britain, under the auspices of the HFEA, to create a human being solely as a means to the end of research. A boundary has been crossed when IVF embryos are intentionally produced with their destruction in mind.

Cloning for research/transplantation further extends the message that the 1990 legislation carried. The highly dehumanising method of production for clones is here compounded by the use of the clone as a mere resource. The practice of producing clone embryos as a mere means to some desired research end would institutionalise the commodification of early human life. Where such commodification is allowed, it becomes difficult to see why destructive or invasive experiments should not be allowed on human beings at later stages of existence. For example, some are already proposing deliberately growing clone children to the foetal stage, then aborting them so that tissue can be extracted from the dead baby. The New Jersey Senate recently passed a bill (Bill S1909) which would allow not only for cloning human beings, but also for implanting them into a uterus at the embryonic stage, then harvesting and killing them for research *at any time from the embryonic period up to the ninth month of gestation*. The logic that denies the humanity of early embryos inexorably extends all the way up to nine month babies. There is no logical reason why the denial should not extend beyond nine months to children, adults and the elderly.

Experimental cloning explicitly endorses the idea that human embryos are mere products. To hold, as many do, that experimental cloning is somehow more morally acceptable than live-birth cloning is to hold a nonsensical position. For whereas the latter, in theory if not in practice, need not involve the killing of a human being, the former very definitely does. Moreover, the very technology developed for experimental cloning will be of great assistance to those who wish to clone for birth.

As we saw earlier, the distancing and imbalance between parents and their IVF offspring is increased a further step with cloning. When the purpose of cloning is destructive embryo research the control exercised over the clone embryo is total. It is deprived of a genuine genetic parent; it is made to order; it is destroyed to order; and it has no natural defenders in the same way that an IVF embryo theoretically has. This further corruption of the relation between parents and their children, and reinforcement of the idea that one generation can reduce the next to the status of raw material for their health/scientific projects, dulls our sensibilities with regard to the dignity and worth of early human beings. Given the remarkable capacity of human beings to get used to procedures which had only recently filled them with repugnance, it is vital to remind ourselves of the importance of human dignity and of our duties to the most vulnerable members of our society.

With regard to human dignity, the philosopher Immanuel Kant famously held that one should act always in such a way that another person is the end and not merely the instrument of one's action. Destructive embryo research turns that principle on its head. By excluding from the principle certain categories of human beings, we undermine the very basis for justice in our society. A just society is one which values human beings not for certain arbitrary features they may possess, but because they are members of the human family.

Complicity problems

Destructive cloning for embryo research creates problems concerning complicity with the practice. To commission or authorise somebody to do destructive embryo research is to intend that activity to take place, and is as indefensible as actually doing it.

If cloning for research/transplantation became widely practised, would doctors who disapprove of creating and killing clone embryos be put under pressure to use treatments derived from the practice? One can imagine a case where a patient with Parkinson's disease requests that a scientist make a clone of him in the belief that embryonic stem cells harvested from the clone could help him. Would a doctor be under a duty to help the patient subsequently with the stem cells obtained from the clone? Would medical guidelines condemn the doctor to refer the patient to a fellow doctor willing to carry out the patient's wish? A patient who wishes to have himself cloned so that embryonic stem cells can be harvested, destructively, from his clone embryo intends that human embryo's death, as, in all likelihood, do all those who knowingly participate in the operation. Consider also how women could be put under pressure by sick relatives to donate their eggs in order for clones to be made. The situation for such women would be agonising, for by donating their eggs they would be participating in acts destructive of human beings.

Experimental cloning might result in increased knowledge about embryonic stem cells in general. Many patients suffering from severe illnesses and desperately seeking a cure for them might be persuaded to use embryonic stem cell treatments developed with the aid of such research. While they would not necessarily be *intending* the destructive acts of scientists in the recent past in doing cloning experiments and embryo research, by the very acceptance of a treatment based on the production and destruction of human beings, they appear to condone a gravely immoral practice. The immorality of the practice is likely to be entwined with other immoral practices, such as the obtaining of large amounts of ova from aborted foetuses. A doctor being asked to help such a patient is being asked to implicitly approve of a practice or practices he or she may rightly regard as inhuman. Such research thereby corrupts the relationship between doctor and patient.

If embryonic stem cells obtained via cloning for research/transplantation were ever to become widely used in medical practice, much pressure would be put on the consciences of those medics who objected to the way in which they were obtained. The lack of protection for pro-life doctors given by the 'conscience clause' of the

1967 Abortion Act should give pause for thought to those who blithely propose similar clauses in relation to legislation on cloning.

At present, as we saw in chapter 1, embryonic stem cell treatments appear to have little future. This is not the case with the ethical alternative, namely using adult stem cells for treatment. However, the pursuit of embryonic stem cell research via human cloning, which the present British government encourages, could open the door to threatening the consciences of people in the healthcare professions, placing them in intolerable situations.

Conclusion

Technological advancement and improvements in medicine have relieved much suffering in this world. Such developments make sense only if ordered to the good of the human race. That race contains in it all who are members of the human kind, all whose very being has inherent dignity, which demands the greatest respect. The Christian knows the ultimate source of that dignity. He or she knows that we are made in God's image, and that each of us is uniquely precious in His eyes. As part of a witness to that truth, we must always argue against developments such as human cloning and oppose all legislation that advances or permits the practice. If there is ignorance about the morality of human cloning it is all the more necessary for those opposed to cloning to educate, with firmness and compassion, those who fail to see the moral problems it involves.

The dignity and value of human bodily life is such that we regard bodily health as a great good. Those suffering from serious illnesses rightly seek for cures for their condition. While their end is good, those proposing to use means destructive of other human beings in order to achieve it essentially reject the idea that it is better to suffer evil than to do it. When there are ethical alternatives for potential treatments, showing much more promise than unethical proposals, there is even less excuse to choose wrongly.

In the same way, those couples suffering from infertility should be assisted in their plight, but only in ways that genuinely help to restore fertility or allow the couple to have a family in other morally acceptable ways. Fostering or adoption, or, perhaps, forms of assisted reproduction which do not replace the conjugal act are humane ways in which such a couple might be helped.

The Christian knows that bodily life, in its earthly state, is not an absolute good. A healthy body is a great good, but its idolisation can lead to great evil. In any human life there will be suffering, both physical and mental. That is part of our fallen condition. God had not wished for us to suffer and die: the misuse of His gifts introduced into the world suffering and death. But from that suffering God draws great goods. For the sufferer there is the possibility of growth in virtue, a coming closer to God and neighbour. Others can find in themselves a call to selflessness and compassion when faced with a suffering person. We must always show solidarity with those who suffer, recognising that there are some difficulties in this life that medicine and technology cannot solve. When this is the case, our duty to lovingly care for the sufferer is evident. To seek to bypass that difficult duty through solutions which degrade others is to degrade ourselves.

GLOSSARY

Abortion Act (1967): Act passed by Parliament in England, Wales and Scotland legalising abortion.

Adult cell donor: anyone donating a cell for the purpose of cloning.

Adult stem cells: stem cells that can be found in specific tissue in the more developed human being (including the developed foetus and newborn baby).

Alzheimer's disease: a brain disorder resulting in a gradual decline in mental and physical abilities.

Artificial insemination: injection of semen into a woman's vagina.

Asexual reproduction: reproduction not involving the fusion of male and female gametes.

Blastocyst: a 5-7 day old embryo.

Choriocarcinoma: a type of cancer unique to humans.

Chromosomes: microscopic bodies in the nuclei of cells containing the genes.

Cloning: the production of a genetic copy of a pre-existing human being (or other organism).

Cloning for birth: as above, but where the aim is to bring the clone to birth by implanting it in a womb.

Cloning for research/transplantation: cloning where the aim is to extract cells from or observe the clone embryo (or perhaps to implant, grow, and destructively extract cells from the clone individual at the foetal stage of development).

Commissioning mother: a woman who commissions/pays for a child to be conceived on her behalf.

Commodification: treating something (or someone) which is not a commodity as if it were one.

Conception: the beginning of a new human life.

Congregation for the Doctrine of the Faith: the Vatican body concerned with safeguarding and developing Church teaching.

Conscience clause: a clause in law or contract exempting persons with conscientious objections.

Contingent: dependent on events; not yet known.

Contraception: the intentional rendering of an otherwise fertile sexual act infertile.

Crohn's disease: inflammation and ulceration of various parts of the intestine.

Culture: the experimental growth of organisms or cells in a nutrient substance. The term is used as a noun to refer to the nutrient substance itself.

Diploid: having paired chromosomes so that the full complement are present (46 in normal human body cells).

DNA: the chemical of which genes are made. It is self-replicating and responsible for the transmission of hereditary characteristics from parents to offspring.

Egg donors: women who donate/sell their ova.

Embryo: The first stage of development of a human being: from conception until the end of the eighth week.

Embryonic stem cells: stem cells culled from an embryo or early foetus.

Embryonic stem cell lines: cells derived from an embryonic stem cell.

Embryo splitting: dividing the early embryo into two or more identical embryos and allowing them to develop autonomously.

Enhancement: the attempt to improve a human being by means of a technical, non-medical intervention.

Enucleated ovum: an ovum with its nucleus removed.

Ex nihilo: from nothing.

Experimental cloning: see cloning for research/transplantation.

Fertilisation: the union of sperm and ovum to generate a new human being.

Foetal cells: cells extracted from a human being at its foetal stage of development.

Foetus: an unborn human being between the age of eight weeks and birth.

Gametes: reproductive cells: sperm in men, ova in women.

Genes: the basic biological units of heredity, made of DNA. They are situated on chromosomes, and come in pairs, as do chromosomes themselves.

Genetic engineering: the alteration of the DNA of a cell for purposes of research, medical treatment or genetic enhancement.

Genetic imprinting: a mechanism in which gene expression depends upon parental origin.

Genetic replica: an organism with identical or near identical genes to another.

Genetic screening: testing for a genetic condition.

Genome: the genetic makeup of a cell.

Gestational mother: a woman pregnant with a baby who is not necessarily the genetic mother (e.g. in the case of cloning where the ovum was provided by another woman).

Haploid: having a single set of unpaired chromosomes (applied to gametes).

Helsinki Accords: declarations of moral principles regulating medical or other research on human subjects.

Human Fertilisation and Embryology Authority (HFEA): A statutory body which regulates, licenses and collects data on fertility treatments and human embryo research in the UK.

Identical twins: human beings or other organisms with identical genes arising from a single zygote.

Immune response: the body's rejection of foreign cells or organs introduced into it.

Immune system: an organism's ability to resist disease and respond to foreign materials.

Immunity tolerance: the body's tolerance to cells or organs introduced into it.

Infallibility: the authority given by God to the Pope and Bishops to teach without error on faith and morals in certain situations.

IVF (*in vitro fertilisation*): The fertilisation of an ovum outside a woman's body in a glass dish. Sometimes babies formed in this manner are referred to as 'test-tube' babies.

Large Offspring Syndrome: a genetic abnormality resulting in oversized foetuses which is dangerous to the foetus and mother.

Live-birth cloning: see cloning for birth.

Miscarriage: spontaneous or accidental expulsion of an unborn child from the mother's body before viability.

Mitochondrial disease: disease related to abnormalities in mitochondrial genes.

Mitochondrial genes: genes in the mitochondria outside the cell nucleus.

Molecular signals: external signals used to coax embryonic stem cell lines to produce specific mature cell types.

Moral intuition: immediate knowledge of, or belief in, a moral proposition.

Motor neurone disease: a progressively degenerative disease causing muscle weakness and wasting.

Nonsexual reproduction: reproduction achieved not through the sexual act between man and woman but nonetheless involving a male and female gamete.

Nucleus: the central part of the cell, containing most of the cell's DNA.

Nuremberg Code: code laid down in 1947 aimed at protecting vulnerable populations from harmful medical experimentation.

Ovary: one of two female reproductive organs producing ova.

Ovulation: the production and discharge of ova from an ovary.

Ovum (plural ova): the egg or female reproductive cell, which can be fertilised by male sperm to form an embryo, or can be enucleated and fused with an adult cell to form a clone embryo.

Papal encyclical: a letter written to the whole Church by the Pope.

Parkinson's disease: a progressive chronic disorder of the central nervous system.

Parthenogenesis: a type of reproduction in which the unfertilised ovum is directly triggered to create a new individual.

Parthenote: individual formed by parthenogenesis.

Placenta: the foetal organ formed in the uterus from which the foetus gets its nourishment.

Pluripotent: stem cells capable of giving rise to almost all of the cell types of the body.

Quasi-genetic mother: gestational mother of a clone not created from one of her adult cells. Quasi because her only genetic contribution to the child will be mitochondrial genes.

Quiescent: inactive.

Randomising: the random distribution of a full set of genes into the (haploid) gametes during their formation from diploid cells.

Reprogramming: the way in which the male and female sets of DNA are prepared for the specific pattern of gene expression required for normal embryo development.

Somatic cell nuclear transfer: the fusion of an adult cell, or the nucleus from that cell, with an enucleated ovum to produce a clone of the adult cell donor.

Specialisation: the process by which cells become adapted to specific functions - and are then known as specialised cells.

Somatic cell: any of the cells of an organism except the reproductive cells.

Sperm: the male reproductive cell. When sperm fertilises an ovum an embryo is created.

Stem cell: an undifferentiated cell giving rise to specialised cells.

Superovulation: result of a hormone treatment to induce ovulation with a view to producing a number of ova in one menstrual cycle.

Surrogate mother: a woman who becomes pregnant with the intention of relinquishing the child to another.

Tautology: the use of words that merely repeats elements of the meaning already conveyed.

Teratoma: a tumour composed of tissue foreign to the site of growth.

Therapeutic: curative.

Tissue biopsy: extraction and examination of cells from living tissue.

Totipotent: stem cells capable of differentiation and of forming a new individual, or any tissue or organ of that individual.

Trophoblast: a membrane enclosing the embryo that becomes attached to the wall of the uterus and provides the embryo with nourishment.

Unspecialised: cells which are not yet adapted to specific functions.

Viable: capable of surviving (outside the womb).

Zygote: the embryo at the single-cell stage.

Further Reading

Church documents

Most of these documents are available from the Catholic Truth Society.

Evangelium Vitae (The Gospel of Life) 1995.
Donum Vitae (Instruction on Respect for Human Life in its Origin and on the Dignity of Human Procreation) 1987.
Catechism of the Catholic Church 1994.
Familiaris Consortio (Regarding the role of the Christian family in the modern world) 1981.
Pontifical Council for the Family *Truth and Meaning Of Human Sexuality* Catholic Truth Society, 1996.

Bioethics texts

Kass, L. 'The Wisdom of Repugnance' in Pence G.E. *Flesh of My Flesh: The Ethics of Cloning Humans* Rowman & Littlefield, 1998.
Correa, J and Sgreccia, E (eds.) *Human Genome, Human Person and the Society of the Future*, Libreria Editrice Vaticana, 1999.
Finnis, J. 'Some fundamental evils in generating human embryos by cloning' in Mazzoni, C.M.(ed.) *Etica della Ricerca Biologica* Leo. S. Olschki, 2000.
Braine, D. 'The Human and the Inhuman in Medicine' in Gormally, L. (ed.) *Moral Truth and Moral Tradition* Four Courts Press, 1994.
Garcia, J.L.A. 'Human Cloning: Never and Why Not' in Mackinnon, B. (ed.) *Human Cloning: Science, Ethics and Public Policy* University of Illinois Press, 2002.

Websites

www.linacre.org
www.stemcellresearch.org
www.lifeissues.net
www.cbhd.org
www.cloninginformation.org